NIKON Z5

CAMERA GUIDE

A Complete Walkthrough guide on camera Nikon Z5

Stephen Gody

Contents

INTRODUCTION

If you are a Nikon Z5 user or considering purchasing one, "The Nikon Z5 Guide" could be a valuable resource for you. It covers a range of topics, including camera part, settings, shooting techniques, lens recommendations and tips are all tailored specifically to this camera model.

The Nikon Z5 is usually the best bang-for-your-buck stills-oriented camera. Image quality from its 24MP sensor is just tad behind class-leading and much of its design, from the build-quality to the ergonomics.

Autofocus performance is also solid; reliable face and eye detect make it a great choice for documenting family/friends, it's also give Full HD capture with the added benefit of in-body image stabilization for hand-held shooting

The Nikon Z5 is an FX-format mirror less camera with a well-rounded feature-set to suit your capture. Its 24.3MP CMOS sensor and EXPEED 6 processor afford wide sensitivity to ISO 51200, quick shooting at 4.5 fps, and UHD 4K video at 30 fps.

Complementing the sensor and processor is a sleek but versatile physical design that includes a magnesium alloy chassis with a weather-sealed construction to suit working in inclement weather.

A high-resolution 3.6m-dot OLED electronic viewfinder allows for high-res eye-level viewing while a rear 3.2" 1.04m-dot tilting touch screen LCD accommodates working from high and low angles.

It's also easy sharing, built-in Wi-Fi and Bluetooth work in conjunction with the Nikon Snap Bridge app for wirelessly transferring photos and videos and remotely controlling the camera from your mobile device.

Chapter 1:

NIKON Z5 CAMERA PARTS

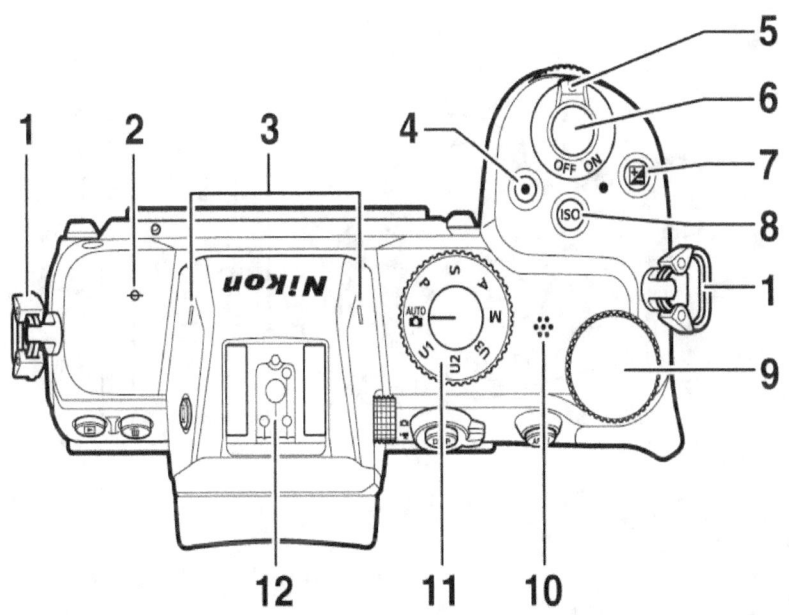

i.   Eyelet

ii.   Focal mark

iii.   Stereo Microphone

iv.   Record Button

v.   Power Switch

vi.   Shutter Release Button

vii.   Exposure Compensation Button

viii.   IOS Button

Fig 2

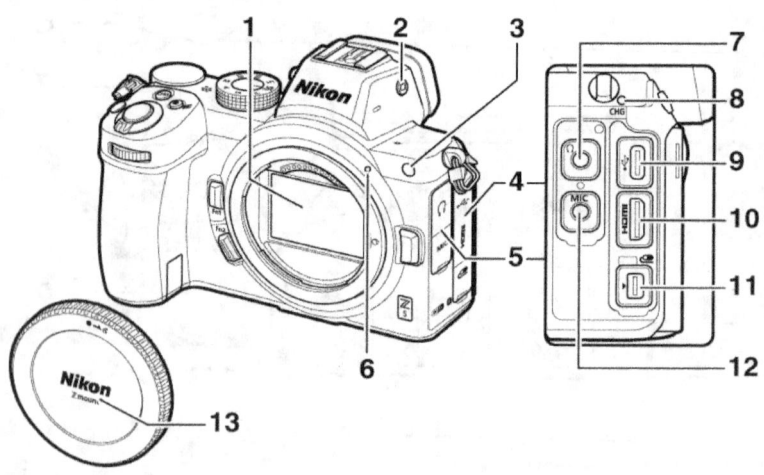

1) Image sensor

2) M button (Monitor Mode)

3) AF-assist illuminator

4) Cover for Accessory Terminal and USB and HDMI connectors

5) Cover for headphone and microphone connectors

6) Lens mounting mark

7) Headphone Connector (Headphone Volume)

8) Charge lamp (Charging AC Adapters)

9) USB connector (Connecting to Computers Via USB)

10) HDMI connector (Connecting to HDMI Devices)

11) Accessory terminal

12) Connector for external microphone

13) Body cap (Attaching a Lens)

Fig 3:

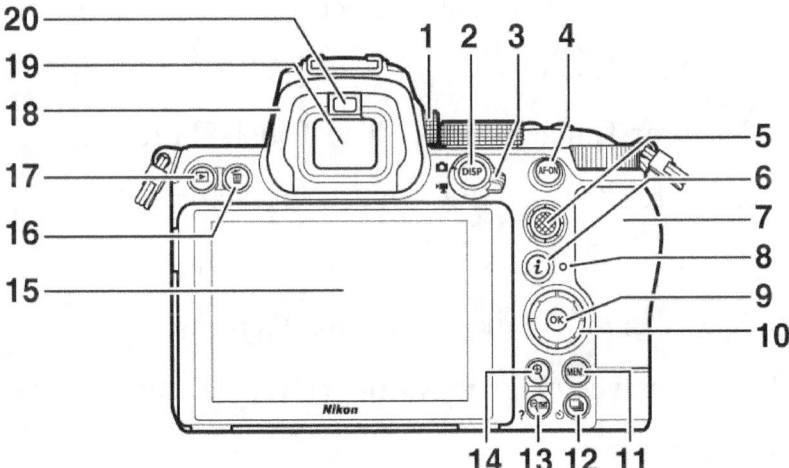

1) Diaper adjustment control

2) DISP button

3) Photo/movie selector

4) AF ON button

5) Sub-selector

6) I button

7) Memory card slot cover

8) Memory card access lamp

9) J button

10) Multi selector

11) G button

12) The c/E (Release Mode/Self-Timer) Button

13) The X and W Viewing Pictures, Using Playback Zoom

14)]X button for Manual Focus, Viewing Pictures, Playback Zoom

15) Monitor Touch Controls, The Touch Shutter

16) O button for Deleting Unwanted Pictures, Deleting Pictures)

17) K button for Playback, Viewing Pictures

18) Rubber eyecup for Viewfinder Eyepiece Accessories

19) Viewfinder

20)   Eye sensor

Fig 4:

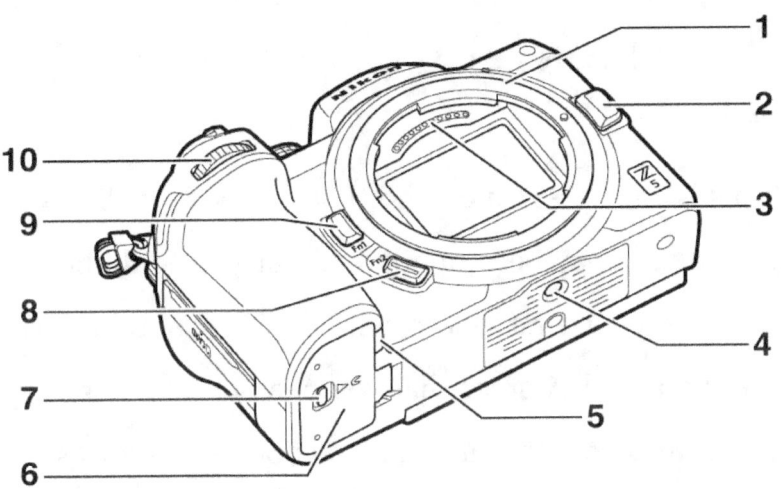

1) Lenses mount (Attaching a Lens, The Focal Plane Mark and Flange-Back Distance).

2) Lens release button (Detaching Lenses)

3) CPU contacts

4) Tripod socket

5) Power connector cover (Attaching a Power Connector and AC Adapter)

6) Battery-chamber cover

7) Battery-chamber cover latch

8) Fn2 button (Focus)

9) Fn1 button (White Balance)

10) Sub-command dial aperture, door, and crevice at your disposal.

CHAPTER 2:

NIKON Z5 CAMERA SETTINGS

If this is your first time of getting this type of Nikon z5 camera you may be thinking of what you to do before you take your first photo with it. This outlines will show you the key steps that you need to take to set-up your camera for the first time so you're ready to start shooting.

Charging the Battery

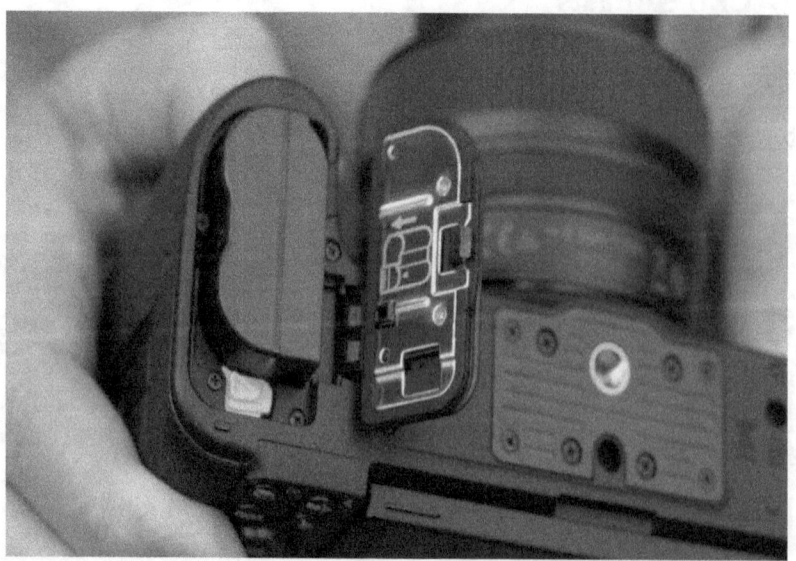

What you need to do first is to charge the battery Before you can perform any task with your camera,. If your camera was supplied with a battery charger, pop the battery in it and connect it to the mains to start charging.

An increasing number of camera batteries are charged via a USB connection and in some cases, there's no battery charger included in the box with the camera. If this is the case for you, put the battery in the camera and find the right cable in the box to connect your camera to a USB charging port.

Memory Card Formatting

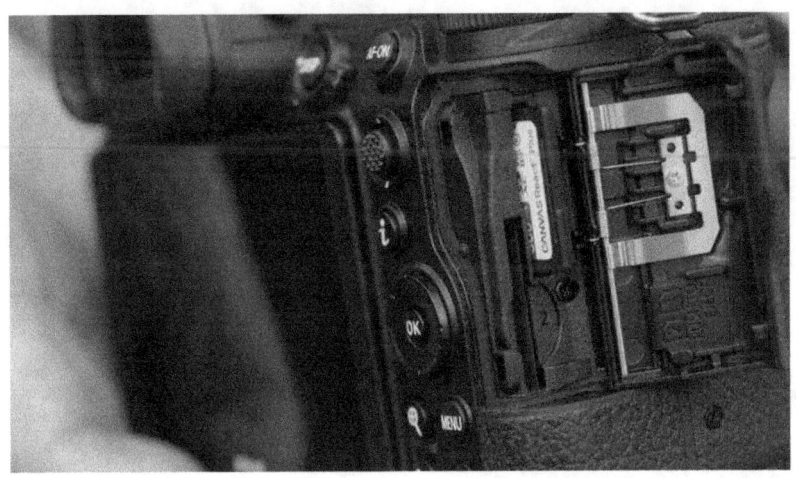

Anytime you get yourself a brand new camera and a brand-new memory card, the best thing for you to do is to format the card as soon as you've inserted it in the camera. Formatting the card deletes any file on it and gets it ready to start work with your camera.

In case you are using an old card that already has images or files on it, make sure you've backup every file on it before you insert the card in the camera and format it.

To format the memory card simply press your camera's menu button, find the Format option and follow the on-screen directions.

Image Quality and Size Setting

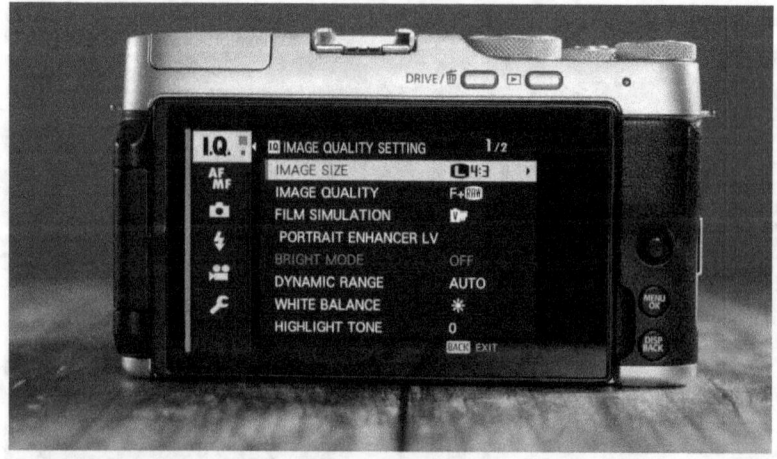

If you want to get the best from your new camera, make sure you use the camera's menu system to set the image quality to Extra Fine or Highest Quality JPEG, and then set the size to Large.

This may consume more space on the memory card you just formatted? Sure! You'll burn through more storage space, but isn't the reason you upgraded to a DSLR or interchangeable lens camera because you wanted to take better quality images?

You can also try your hand at processing raw files, if you want. These files capture more detail and generally produce better results, but they have to be processed and converted to Jpegs before you can share them.

These days the raw conversion software that's supplied free with your camera is usually made available via a download link rather than as a disk in the box. Have a look through the paperwork in the box, or search the manufacturer's website to find the correct link.

You can also use third-party image-editing software, such as Capture One Pro, DxO Optics Pro or

Photoshop Elements, but you will need to make sure that your camera's raw files are supported.

You can even set your new camera to shoot raw and JPEG images simultaneously. We'd recommend at this stage that you don't just shoot raw files exclusively.

Sensitivity Setting (ISO)

Setting your camera's sensitivity, or ISO setting, determines how much light your camera needs to take a photo.

High sensitivity settings such as ISO 6400 are handy for shooting in low-light conditions, but the higher your ISO setting, the more noise will creep into your images. Low settings in the ISO range produce the best-quality images but they can only be used when there is lots of light.

In these early stages of your photographic journey it's probably best to set your camera's sensitivity to automatic and let the camera decide which is best.

Setting the White Balance

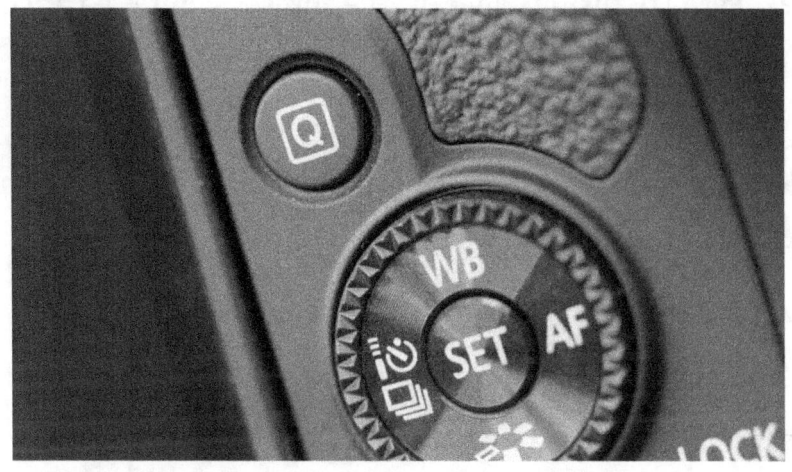

Same as sensitivity, your new camera's automatic white balance (AWB) setting is probably the best starting point at this stage. Your camera is generally pretty accurate and should produce images with natural colors and neutral tones in most types of conditions.

Once you've grown more confident with using your camera's controls you can begin to experiment with the white balance settings that are designed for specific lighting conditions. You can even take full control and try setting a manual value!

Therefore, if your camera isn't giving the colors you expect, try using one of the preset white balance settings and check out the result.

The Metering Mode Check

Setting your camera to its Evaluative, Matrix or Multi-zone/segment metering, which is a good general-purpose mode that will suggest the most practical exposure settings in most conditions?

If you're using a mirrorless camera, its viewfinder and screen can preview the impact of the camera settings that are selected, so you'll see if the image is going to be too dark or too bright and adjust the exposure compensation accordingly.

Focus Mode Setting

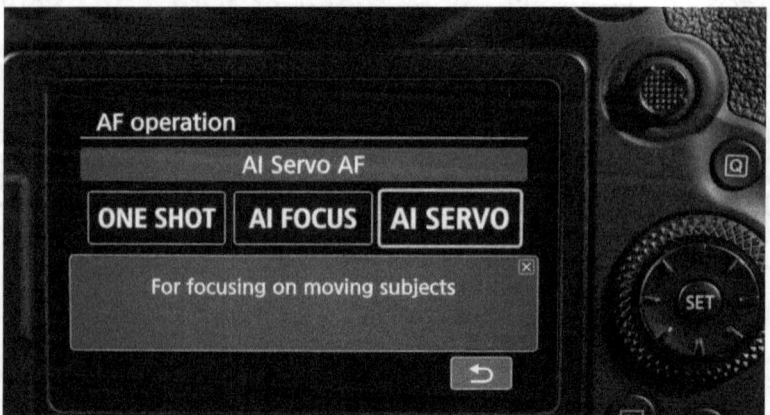

You can set the focus mode to be working automatically by using the camera's autofocus (AF) system, or can be used manually by rotating the lens's focus ring with your hand, but you need to let the camera know which method you intended to use. When autofocus is selected, the camera will try to focus on whatever subject is sitting under the selected AF point.

Check the camera over to see if there's a control to set the focus mode directly, or press the menu button and locate the focus mode control. You will find that there are two (or sometimes more) AF options, Single AF and Continuous AF (AI Servo on Canon cameras) mode.

Note, we suggest setting your camera to its Single AF mode. This setting focuses your lens when you half-press the shutter release button.

Setting the Drive Mode

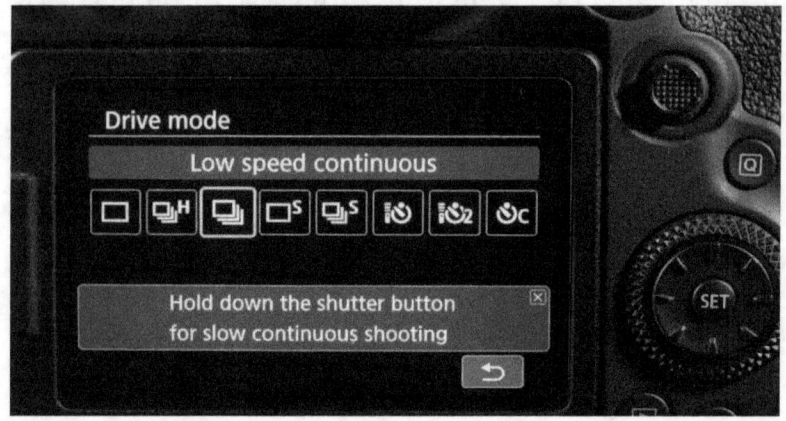

Setting your camera's drive mode is an important control when you're photographing a moving object. Setting the drive mode to its continuous shooting setting will enable you to take a sequence of images in quick succession (you will want to set the camera to Continuous AF mode as well if the subject is moving).

For as long as you keep the shutter release button pressed down (or until the buffer or card becomes full) the continuous shooting mode will allow your camera to keep firing the shutter to capture images.

If you want to capture just one image at a time – which you probably will in most situations – set the Single-shot mode.

Exposure Mode

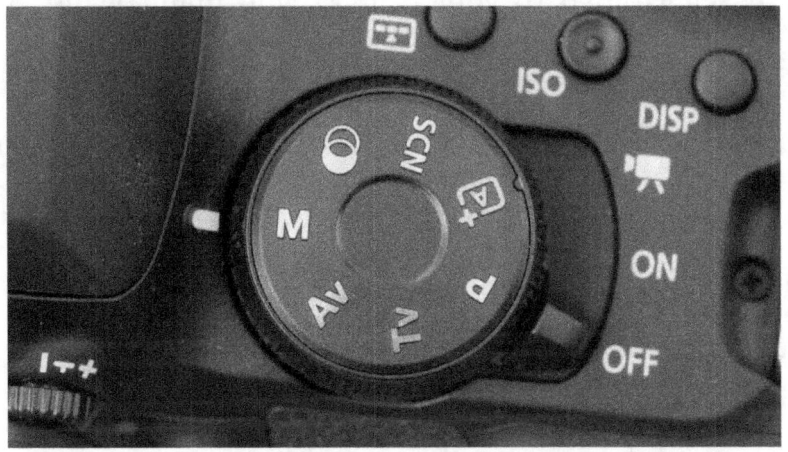

This is the most important setting of it all. Setting your new camera to Automatic (Auto) or Program exposure mode instructs it to decide which shutter speed and aperture settings are best given the lighting conditions.

This can be a great option for beginner photographers who want to concentrate solely on getting their composition right.

Meanwhile, if you want to take charge over your exposure you might want to try one of your camera's Scene mode options, such as Portrait, Landscape or Sport. These modes tailor the exposure and color settings to better suit the subject.

As time goes on, as you are growing more confident and accustomed to your camera, you might want to take even more control by using options like the aperture and shutter priority modes.

Aperture priority mode is when the camera determines the best shutter speed. It's worth remembering that setting a small aperture (which is represented by a large f/number, such as f/22) creates lots of depth of field, which mean a lot of your image will be in focus.

However, a large aperture (which is represented by a small f/number, such as f/2.8) restricts the depth of field so that only a small section of the image on either side of the main focal point is sharp.

Using the same principle as Aperture priority, Shutter priority mode lets you set a desired shutter speed, for example, to freeze a fast-moving subject, and the camera then determines the appropriate aperture setting.

Finally, in Manual exposure mode you take incharge and set both the shutter speed and aperture.

On your Live View screen or in your viewfinder you will find the camera's meter indicator to help guide you. Generally, you want the meter indicator to rest in the middle to provide an even exposure.

CHAPTER 3:

SHOOTING TECHNIQUES

Mode Dial

This is use to choose between shutter speed and aperture so that it can be adjusted manually or are set automatically by the camera. The Mode Dial is listed below.

Auto

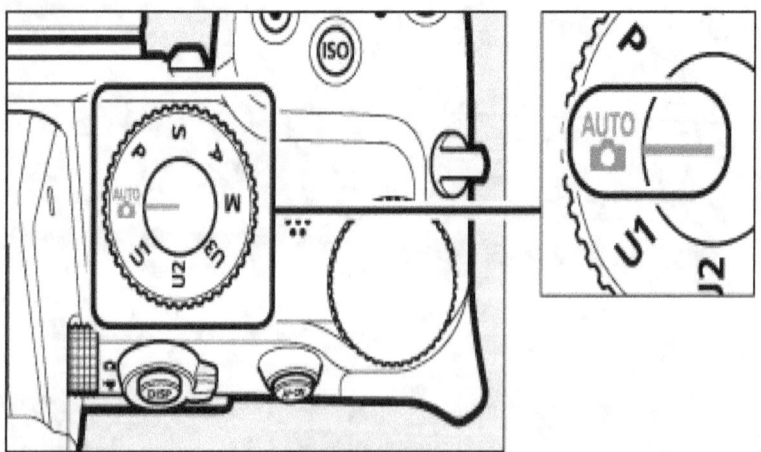

This is the "point-and-shoot" mode, and it allows the camera to handle all the settings (b mode for taking photos, b mode for shooting videos).

Auto (Programmed)

You may set the camera to automatically adjust the shutter speed and aperture based on the built-in software, making sure that it gets the best possible exposure in most situations.

- Turning the primary control dial ("flexible program") allows the user to choose from a variety of shutter speed and aperture settings that provide the same exposure.
- A flexible program indicator (*) is shown while the program is active.
- When the indicator disappears, turning the main command dial will return the shutter speed and aperture settings to their preset values. When the camera is switched off or the mode dial is adjusted to a different setting, the flexible program also terminates.

Priority Auto (Shutter)

- With this setting, you may choose the shutter speed and let the camera adjust the aperture for you. You can "freeze" motion with a rapid shutter speed and imply motion with a slow shutter speed by blurring things in motion.

- To adjust the shutter speed, turn the main command dial.
- You have the option to adjust the shutter speed from 1/8000 s to 30 s, or x200.
- The shutter speed can be fixed to the value you choose.

Automobile with Aperture-Priority

- To get the best possible shot, just choose the aperture in A, and the camera will adjust the shutter speed automatically.
- The sub-command dial allows you to alter the aperture.
- The lens determines the lowest and maximum aperture values.
- The chosen value can be used to lock the aperture.

The manual is labeled M

- When shooting in manual mode, you have complete control over the aperture and shutter speed. Long-time exposures of subjects like fireworks or the night sky can be captured with this mode ("bulb" or "time" photography, long-time exposures).

- The command dials allow you to alter the shutter speed and aperture in relation to the exposure indicators.

- The shutter speed can be adjusted by turning the main command dial. You have the option to select the shutter speed to x200, "bulb," "time," or any value between 1/8000 s and 30 s.

- The sub-command dial allows you to alter the aperture.

- The lens determines the lowest and maximum aperture values.

- The values you choose for the aperture and shutter speed can be locked.

ISO Mode Selector

You can change the camera's light sensitivity (ISO sensitivity) to suit the lighting conditions. Typically, faster shutter speeds at the same aperture are possible with greater values.

Changing the ISO Level

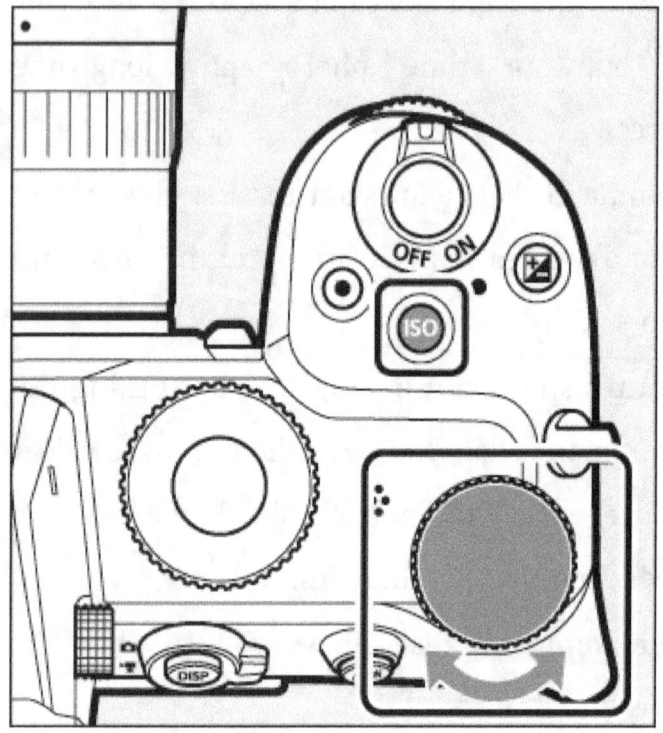

- Manipulate the primary control dial while holding down the S button.

ISO 100 to 51200 are the available values. Along with the standard ISO 100 and 51200 settings, you can also find an extended range of about 0.3 to 1 EV.

- An ISO AUTO option is available in Auto.
- While shooting, the screen will show the currently selected option.

Automated ISO control

When shooting in modes P, S, A, or M, the Auto ISO sensitivity control will make adjustments to the ISO sensitivity if the user's specified setting does not provide appropriate exposure. To avoid having the ISO sensitivity set too high, you have the option to choose an upper limit for the auto ISO sensitivity control (200-Hi 1.0).

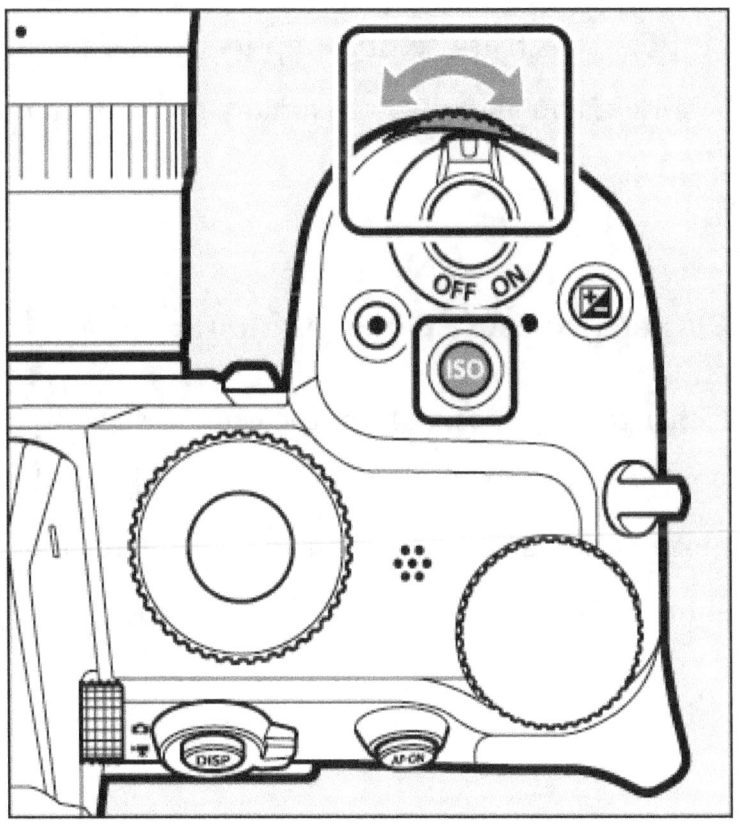

- When you want to toggle the auto ISO sensitivity control on or off, hold down the ISO button and turn the sub-command dial to choose between ISO AUTO and ISO.
- ISO AUTO will appear on the shooting display when the auto ISO sensitivity control is turned on. The displays will also indicate the current ISO sensitivity when the user changes it from the setting they chose.
- The [ISO sensitivity settings] option in the photo shooting menu allows you to modify the maximum sensitivity.

The E-Knob (Exposure Compensation)

- To change the exposure from the camera-suggested value, press this button. You can adjust the exposure of your camera to make your photos look lighter or darker.

Making adjustments to exposure compensation

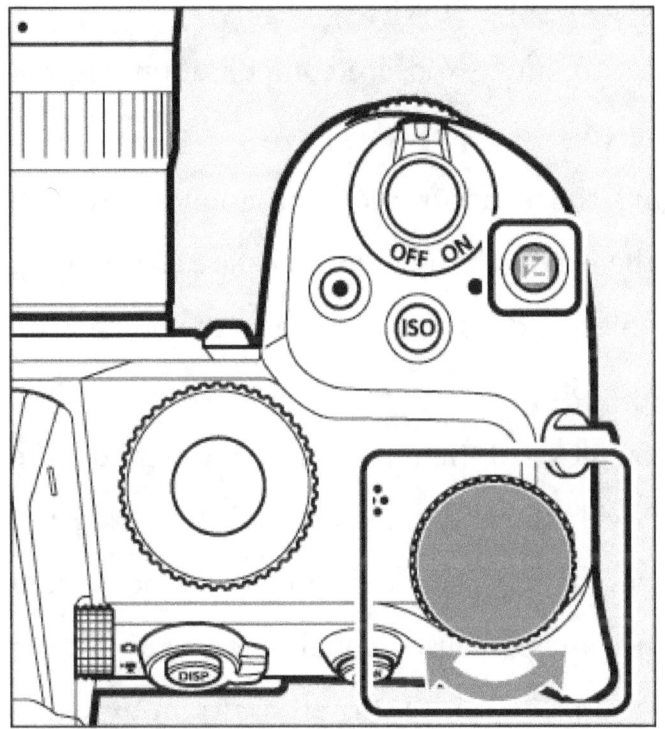

- Turn the primary control dial while holding down the E button.
- Pick a value between -5 EV (being underexposed) and +5 EV (being overexposed). In movie mode, you can choose values between -3 EV and +3 EV.
- By design, modifications are applied in 1/3 EV increments. Using Custom Setting b1 [EV steps for exposure control], you may adjust the increment size to 1/2 EV.

- Lower values result in a darker subject, and higher values in a brighter one.
- When set to auto, exposure compensation will not be activated.
- Changing the exposure compensation to ±o will return the exposure to its normal state. Turning off the camera does not reset the exposure compensation.
- Once you let go of the E button in photo mode, the camera will show an E icon and the exposure indication, or an E icon alone in video mode, when the value is less than or equal to ±o.o. By hitting the E button, you can confirm the current exposure compensation value.

The button labeled "Release Mode/Self-Timer" In this setting; you can customize what happens when you press the shutter button.

Selecting an Execution Mode

Select a release mode using the multi-selector after hitting the green button (c), and then press {ok} to select it.

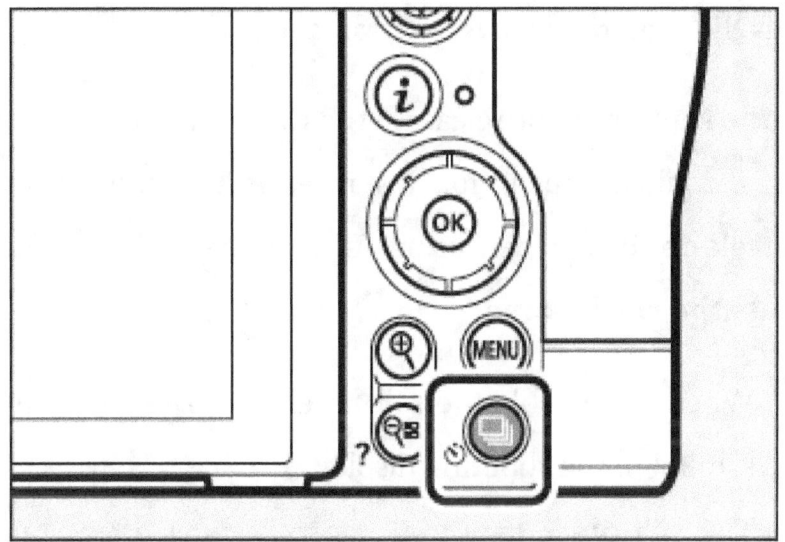

As you shoot, the screen will show you the choice you're now using.

Timer for Yourself

When you're in self-timer mode, you can take a picture as soon as the timer goes off by hitting the shutter release button.

- Use the multi-selector to select [self-timer], then press 3.
- Utilize the multi-selector to select the number of photos and the desired delay before the shutter is released.

Put the camera in focus and frame it.

If the shutter is not released, the timer will not begin. This could happen, for instance, if the camera is unable to focus when using AF S as the focus mode.

Gets the clock going

- When you enable the self-timer, you'll see a timer symbol in the shooting display.
- The self-timer lamp will start flashing after you fully press the shutter-release button to start the timer. Two seconds before the timer goes out, the light stops flashing.

The Sub- Selector

The focus point can be chosen using the sub-selector. Locking exposure and focus can also be done using the sub-selector's center.

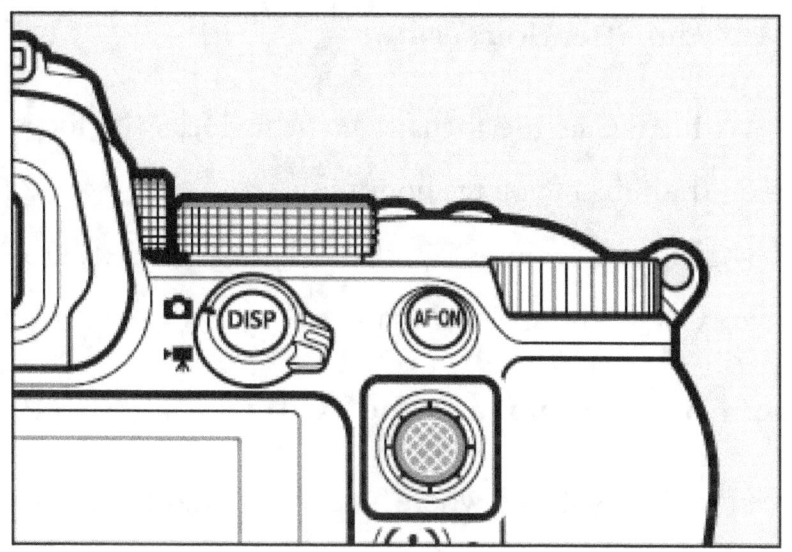

Selection of Emphasis Points

When using an AF-area mode (AF-Area Mode) option other than auto-area AF, this can be utilized to choose the focus point.

The Exposure Lock

- After metering a subject, you can recompose the photo so that it is in the focus region you want, even if it won't be in the final shot.

- Spot and center-weighted metering work best with exposure lock.

Keep your attention secure

- With AF-C as the focus mode, this locks the focus on the subject you're shooting.
- Focus lock requires another AF-area mode; auto-area AF is not one of them.

Capturing the emphasis and lighting

- Place the subject where you want the camera to focus, and then click the shutter release button halfway to adjust the exposure and focus.
- Depress the sub-selector's center.
- When you press the sub-selector's center, focus and exposure will lock. Even if you adjust the composition, the exposure won't vary.
- The monitors will show an AE-L icon. Adjust the shot's composition and press the shutter button while holding down the sub-selector's center.
- Keep the same distance from the item and the camera. Let go of the lock and refocus at the revised distance if the object's distance changes.

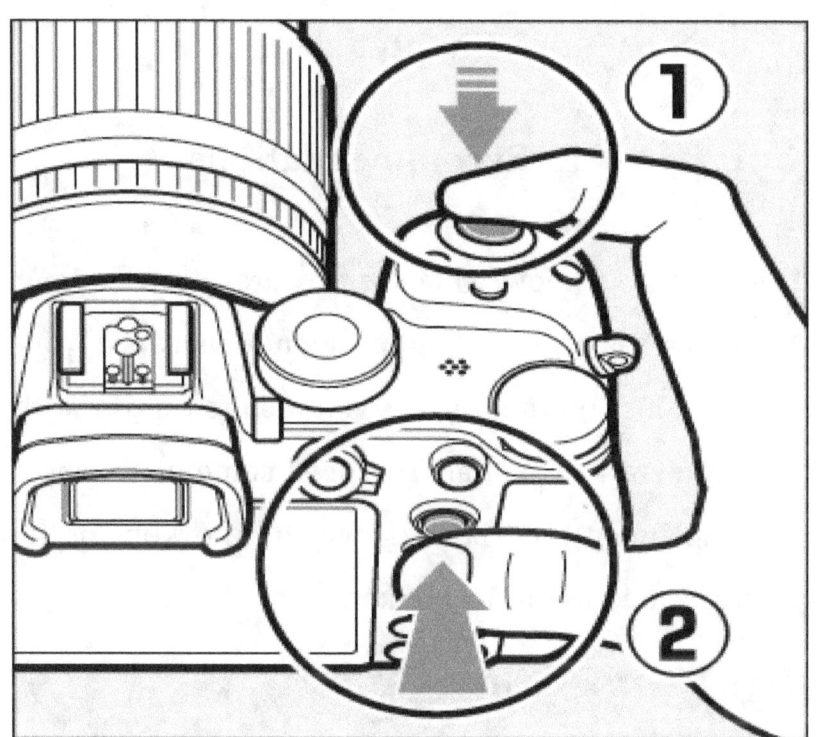

Chapter 4

Lens Recommendations

How can you know which lenses are ideal for your Nikon Z5? Finding a happy medium between your expectations and the subjects you wish to capture with your camera is essential. You need some good lenses to complement the Nikon Z5, which is now one of the greatest cameras on the market.

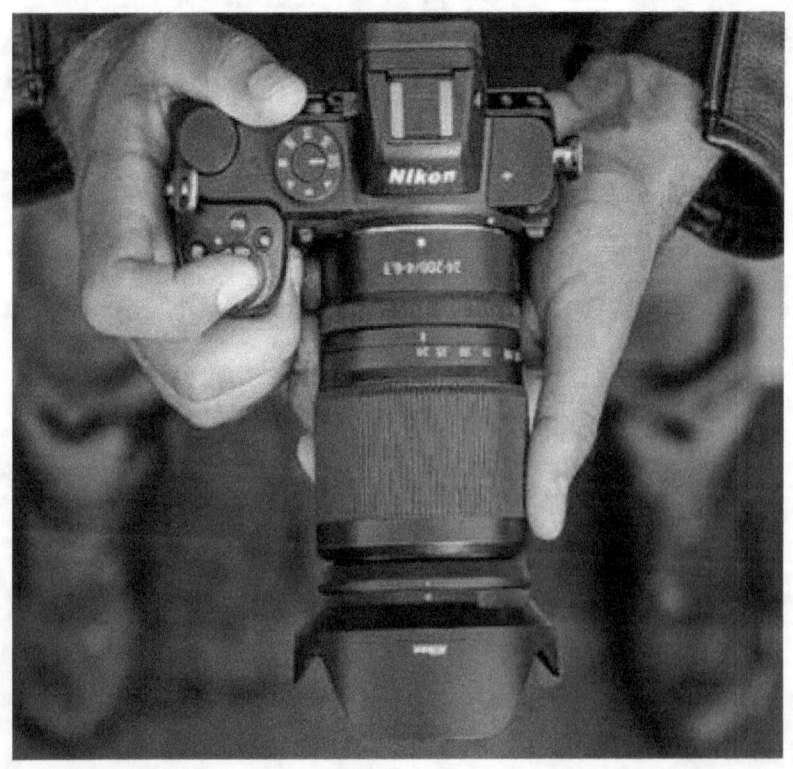

It doesn't take much thought to realize that the two-times zoom range and restricted maximum aperture severely limit the usability of the Nikkor Z 24-50mm f4-6.3 retractable kit lens, which is typically sold with the Nikon Z5. If you're planning to buy lenses with the intention of upgrading to a Nikon Z6 II or Z7 II in the future, or if you're just looking to step up your game, then you should check out this list of the top Nikon Z lenses.

From personal experience with both the camera and its lenses, we have compiled a list of what we believe to be the top Nikon Z5 lenses. Be mindful of a few factors if you want to cover as much ground as possible in terms of focus lengths and shooting styles.

The price of using your Nikon camera for long-distance shots of sports or wildlife quickly rises. Whether you're taking pictures of people, places, or things for fun or for work, the Nikon Z5 is an excellent camera. To get the most out of it, try one of these lenses.

For the Nikon Z 24-70mm f/4 S

The size and weight of this lens are significantly reduced. A lower diameter of the front glass parts and a retractable construction make for compact stowage, but the trade-off is that the f/4 aperture rating transmits less light and doesn't allow for a tight depth of field.

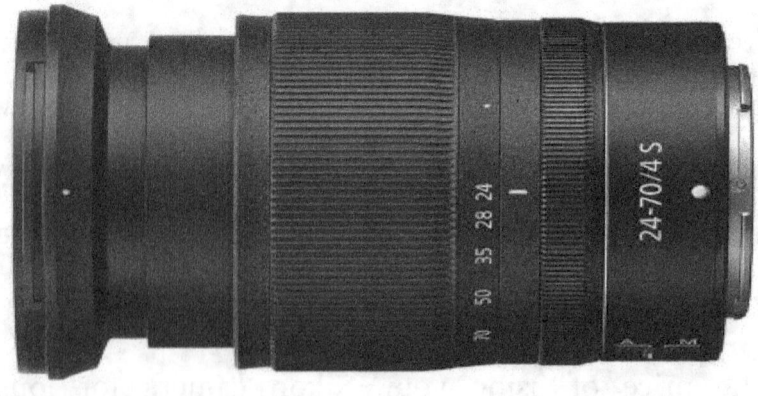

On the other hand, the picture quality is absolutely top-notch. The control ring, typical of Z-mount lenses, allows for a number of customizable capabilities, including step-less aperture adjustment when shooting video, fully manual focusing, and manual override of autofocus.

Nikon Z 24-120mm f/4 S

With a 5x zoom range, the Nikon Z 24-12mm f/4S can reach 120mm, giving you more flexibility than the 24-70mm f/4 lens. Because of this, it is more expensive and heavier, but it is also more versatile. For F-mount DSLRs, Nikon offers the Z 24-120mm f/4 S, a mirrorless take on the classic 5x standard zoom.

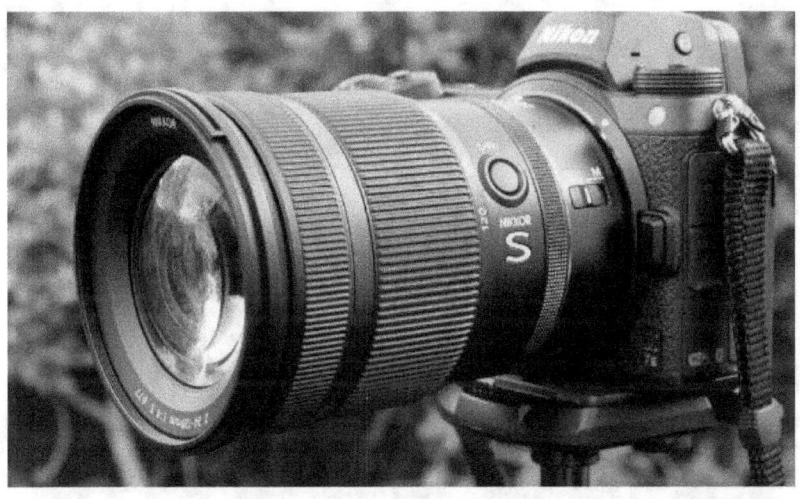

The greater mount circumference and closer proximity to the image sensor of the Z system are both fully utilized for their optical benefits. In the end, you get better clarity and overall image quality across the board and at all zoom levels, all in a relatively small and light body.

The Nikon Z 28-75mm f/2.8

An exquisite lens, the Nikon Z 28-75mm f/2.8 offers a quick conventional zoom with a constant maximum aperture of f/2.8. Although the lens's zoom range is a little strange and its wide-angle end only extends to 28mm, it wowed us during testing, and its compact size makes it ideal for travel.

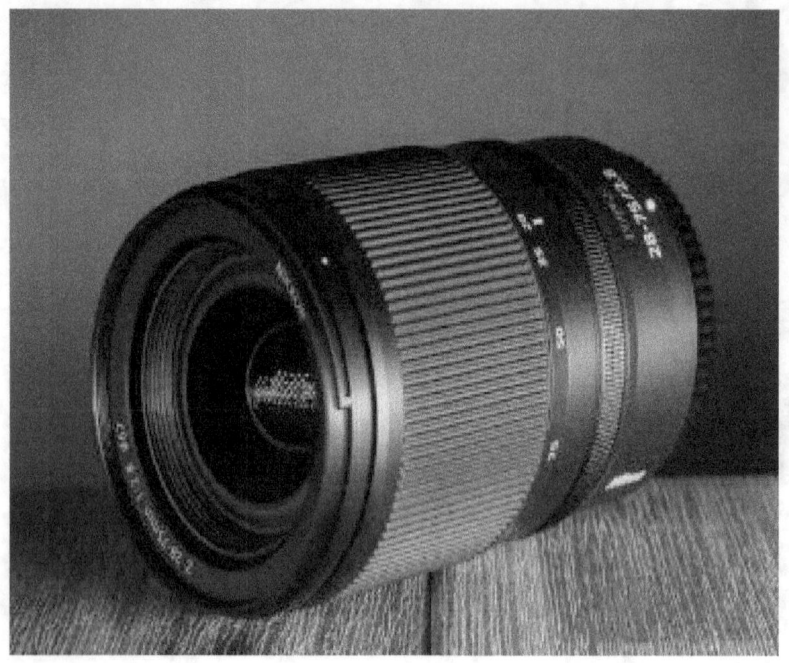

Leica Z 14–30mm f/4 S

When it comes to compactness, affordability, and wider-than-usual fields of view (even for an ultra-wide zoom), the Nikkor Z 14–30mm f/4 S remains the finest match for the Nikon Z5.

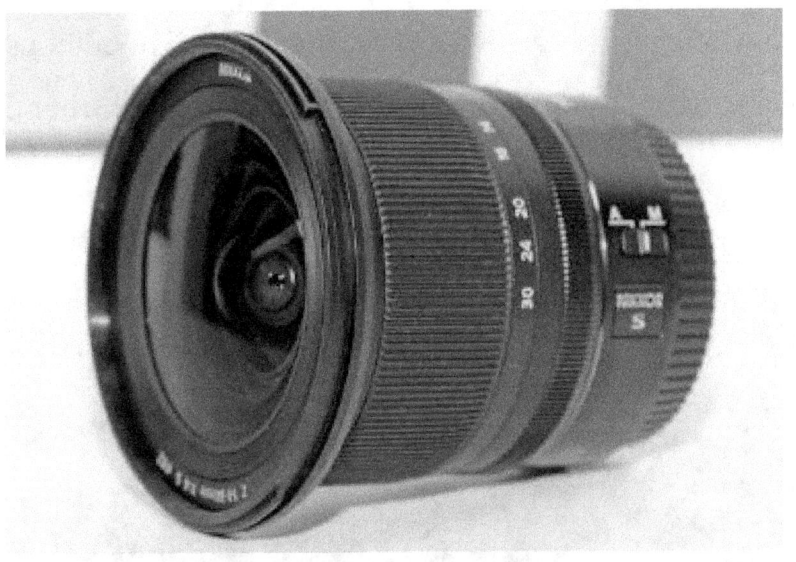

It features quick and almost silent stepping motor autofocus technology and a configurable control ring, as are hallmarks of most S-line lenses. There isn't a physical focus distance scale, and the lens depends on the in-body stabilization system of the Z5 and Z7 II for stabilization rather than having its own internal mechanism.

While this omission may annoy some photographers, it won't bother others. The performance and picture quality are top-notch. The 82mm attachment thread allows for easy filter attachment, and the lens has exceptional corner-to-corner sharpness for its wide-angle design. The hood is retractable for added convenience. Because many wide-angles have bulbous front parts, this is crucial for using filters with them.

A sharp 85mm f/1.8 Nikon lens

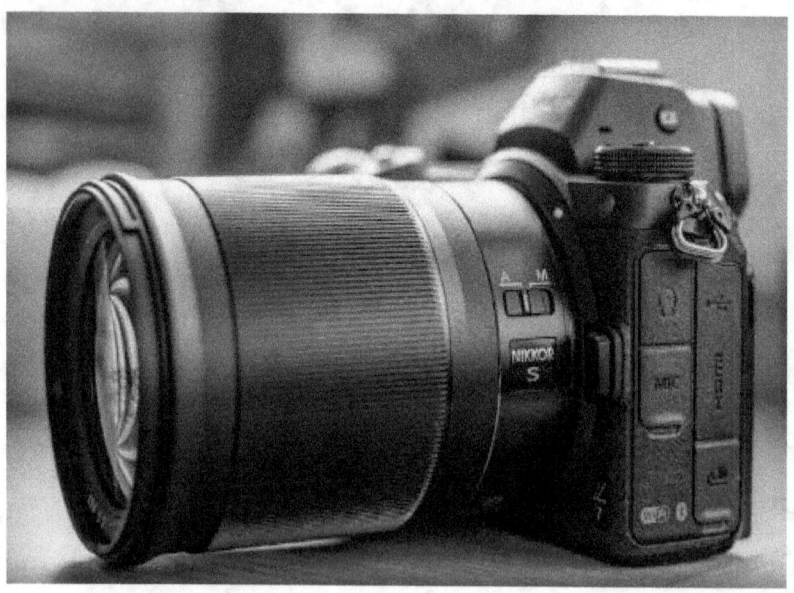

Portraits with blurred backgrounds are a breeze to shoot with a full-frame camera and a fast 85mm lens.

From a comfortable distance, the focal length is perfect for half-length and head-and-shoulder images. As with other Z-mount f/1.8 S-line primes, this lens has excellent build quality and weather seals. The faster 85mm f/1.4 lenses are generally chosen for their narrower depth of field, which helps to blur the background a bit more effectively while highlighting the main subject.

Canon 50mm f/2.8 Nikon Z MC

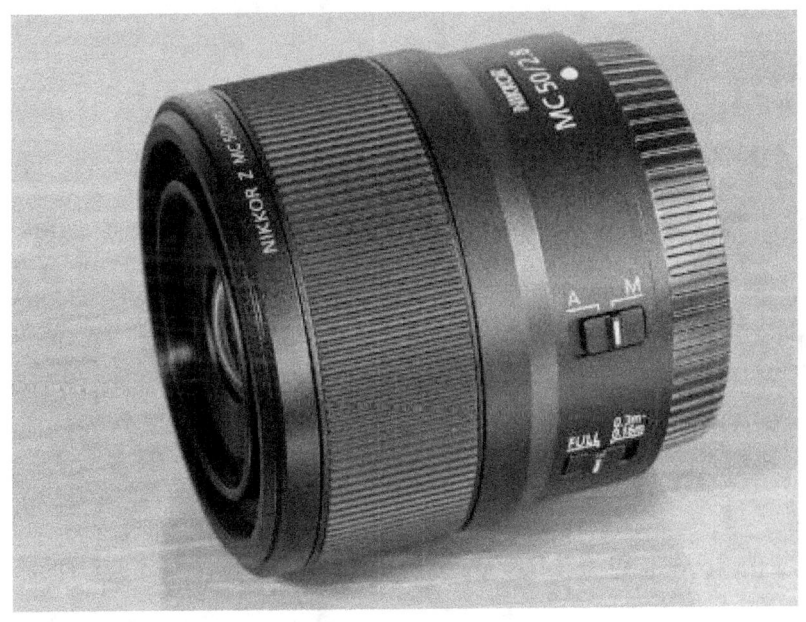

Although it is intended to appeal to Nikon Z5 owners and might double as a general purpose 'standard' prime lens, the Nikkor Z MC 50mm f/2.8 has a lower focal length than other macro lenses. We really like the new Nikkor Z macro lens. It's a great travel companion for a full-frame Z-series body thanks to its lightweight and compact design. The one catch is that you'll need to get rather close to your subject (in this case, no more than 2 inches) in order to get full 1.0x macro magnification.

Sony NEX 24-200mm f/4-6.3 VR

In order to address all of your shooting needs with a single lens, the 24-200mm is your best bet. Landscapes, candid portraits, and everything in between are all within its zoom's purview, which extends from a wide-angle of 24mm all the way to a telephoto of 200mm.

Travelers love these super zoom lenses because they allow them to bring along a single unit and eliminate the hassle of constantly switching lenses.

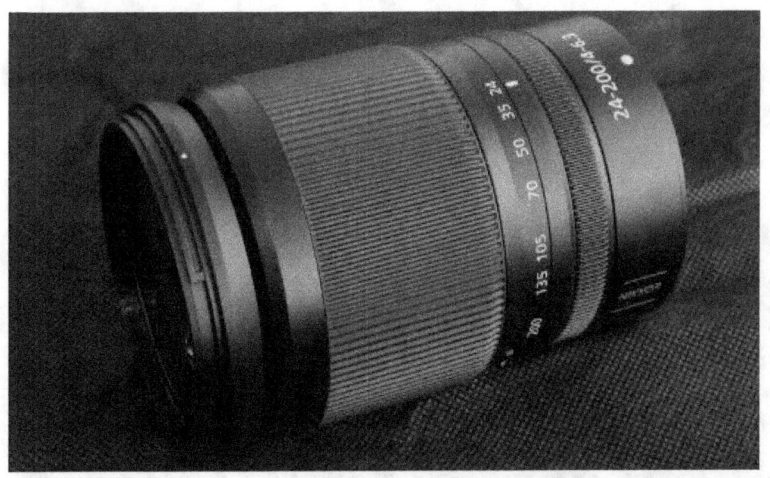

It included regular and telephoto zoom lenses with outstanding picture quality. Its 4.5-stop optical stabilizer is very effective, and its small size and low weight are very appealing. For still images and moving footage, it's your best bet.

View-Master Nikkor Z 100–400mm f/4.5–5.6 VR S

The only real hole in Nikon's lens lineup is the lack of reasonably priced telephotos for full-frame Z-mount cameras like the Z5. Impressive picture quality, fast focusing, and 5.5 stops of VR make this lens a must-have.

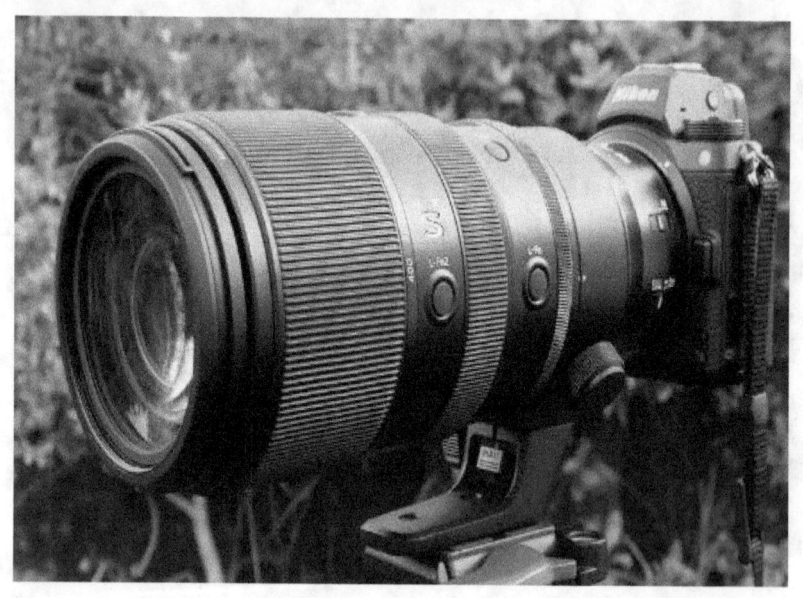

A multi-function OLED display, additional "de-clicked" control rings, and user-adjustable function buttons all contribute to improved handling and top-notch overall performance. A respectable Z-mount successor to the old Nikon AF-S 80-400mm f/4.5-5.6G ED VR lens, which debuted in 2013 with DSLRs in mind, this lens is heavy and expensive, but it does a good job.

Chapter 5

Picture Controls

Select from a wide range of Picture Control options in Nikon's Picture Control, including Standard, Neutral, Vivid, Monochrome, Portrait*, Landscape*, and Flat*. When you put it all together, you can tweak a lot of parameters.

Choose from four modes that let you tweak saturation,sharpness, contrast, brightness, and standard/neutral/vivid/portrait/landscape. Adjusting sharpness, contrast, brightness, filter effects, and tone is made easier with monochrome.

Similar to how photographers used to manipulate film emulsions to get the desired effect, many modern photographers utilize picture controls to add a unique touch to their digital photographs.

Digital cameras from Nikon, such as the Nikon 1 series with interchangeable lenses, COOLPIX point-and-shoot models, and DSLRs, all come with picture controls.

To adjust the picture control, go to the shooting menu and then find the option to select picture control. Highlight Manage Picture Control to install supplementary Picture Controls or establish custom Picture Control settings.

Standard

whether you're shooting portraits, landscapes, or any other kind of photo, the Standard Picture Control will help you achieve uniformly balanced results. Levels of sharpness, contrast, brightness, saturation, and color can be tweaked independently in Standard. Easy, balanced adjustment is made possible using Quick Adjust.

Neutral

Images that are most faithful to the source scene are displayed here. Stay away from overly enhanced images if you want an accurate representation of the subject's distinctive tones and shades.

The overall effect of neutral is more calming than that of standard. Using Neutral, you have the ability to independently modify brightness, contrast, saturation, hue (coloration), and sharpening.

Vivid

With the vibrant, modern-looking photos that have the perfect amount of sharpness and contrast for the subject, when compared to Standard, Vivid gives off a more glitzy vibe. When you want to draw attention to brightly colored clothing, city streets, fruits, or flowers, this is the way to go. Color, saturation, sharpness, contrast, and brightness can all be tweaked separately in Vivid. Easy, balanced adjustments are made possible with Quick Adjust.

Simple color scheme

Shades like black and white or sepia are achieved with monochromatic You may achieve the look of a color filter in black-and-white photos by choosing Filter Effects, and you can mimic the process of working with photographic paper in a darkroom by using Toning to change the overall tone of your images.

On a per-image basis, you can tweak the sharpening, contrast, brightness, toning saturation, filter effect (Y/O/R/G), and monochrome mode.

Selectable image controls

The D3X, D3S, D3, D700, D300S, and D300 DSLRs come with portrait and landscape as optional picture controls, but you may also download them to install them on your own.

Again, verify your handbook because different camera models may have different maximum numbers of optional picture controls. In addition, certain Nikon DSLRs are compatible with picture controls that mimic the style of the D2X and D2XS models.

The Picture Controls page is where you can get the optional controls to download.

Picture perfect

Using neutral as its foundation, Portrait creates skin tones that look more realistic, as if shot on professional-grade film, with a crisp and true finish that gives the impression of depth. Portrait allows you to fine-tune each color, saturation, sharpness, contrast, and brightness independently.

Easy, balanced adjustment is made possible using Quick Adjust.

Landscape

Compared to Standard, this one generates a lot more intensity. Images with rich gradations and increased vibrancy benefit from Landscape's calming, relaxed color palette, which is superior to Vivid for any natural scene.

Sharpening, contrast, brightness, saturation, and hue (coloration) can all be tweaked separately in Landscape. Easy, balanced adjustment is made possible using Quick Adjust.

Flat

Flat maintains the material's properties with minimal exaggeration. The finish lacks contrast and appears less alive when compared to neutral.

When filming video, flat is the most common setting to employ. Oversaturated colors, blocked shadows, or overblown highlights are unusual when post-production video is edited, allowing for a wide range of tonalities in the brightness and color spectrum.

When you are planning to edit the scene after the fact, this mode is ideal because of the wealth of information it provides, from highlights to shadows.

After the release of the Nikon D810 DSLR, the flat picture control became standard on all subsequent models. Picture Control Utility 2 is a feature included in Nikon Capture NX-D, Nikon ViewNX2, and Nikon ViewNX-i software.

It allows users to change the flat picture control on photos. This feature was available as of June 26, 2014, and as of March 2015, respectively.

Easy Modification

Achieving balanced adjustments is made easier using Quick Adjust. An automated five-level adjustment range (-2 to +5) is applied to sharpness, contrast, and saturation.

To enhance the features of each picture control, drag the value to the plus side, and to weaken them, drag it to the minus side.

You can tailor each item to your tastes and obtain the precise results you need after using Quick Adjust by making finer, more detailed adjustments. With the exception of flat, neutral, and monochrome, you can utilize Quick Adjust to make adjustments with every picture control.

Sharpening

Starting at [o] (no sharpening), it gives you ten levels of control over the prominence of your subject's contours. The camera can also be set to "auto" ([A]) to automatically adjust to different shooting circumstances. A lower value will result in a softer image, while a greater value will make it more noticeable.

In stark contrast

By default, the camera will adapt to the lighting and other environmental factors when you set it to [A] (auto). Image tones can be made softer by adjusting to the negative side and harder by moving to the plus side.

On one hand, you have the negative side, which is great for sunny portraits or when you want to avoid blown highlights; on the other hand, you have the positive side, which is ideal for faraway views engulfed in mist. (Contrast cannot be altered until Active D-Lighting is set to OFF.)

Clarity

Only in images can the clarity be changed. Images are softer when the value is lower and clearer when the value is higher; sharpening primarily controls the subject's outlines, and clarity controls the subject's clarity while preserving the gradation of shadow and highlight areas.

You can utilize clarity to make anything that is cloudy appear clear while keeping the details, or to soften something that looks rigid.

Brightness

When adjusting the brightness of the entire image, you have the option to select [-1], [0], or [+1] for deeper black or white gradients. If you set it to [-1], it will make the lightest parts seem darker and the darkest parts darker, and if you set it to [+1], it will make the lightest parts brighter and the darkest parts deeper. (You can't change the brightness unless you turn Active D-Lighting off.)

Saturation in colors other than black and white

From [-3] to [+3], you have seven levels of control over the saturation of photographs. Another option is to press the [A] button, which will cause the camera to automatically adjust to the lighting and subject matter. A gentler degree of brightness is produced by moving toward the negative side, while a deeper brilliance is provided by moving toward the plus side.

Color (outside of black and white)

With its seven-level slider, which goes from [-3] to [+3], you can easily change the color of your photographs. When it comes to skin tones, the negative side brings out more redness, and the positive side brings out more yellow.

Y/O/R filter effects only

Using this feature is like taking color photos through a black-and-white filter. In particular, it highlights the difference between the colors [yellow], [orange], and [red], with the contrast being stronger from [Y] to [O] to [R]. When taking landscape photos, this picture control is useful for reducing the contrast between the sky and the ground.

I exclusively use filter effects in monochrome. Furthermore, it gives the impression of taking black-and-white photos via a green filter.

Monochrome toning

Much like toning photographic paper, it lets you change the overall image's color tones. A default black and white option is one of 10 available colors. Level of saturation for toning (unicolor only) It's basically an extra feature for [B&W], allowing you to change the color shading on seven different levels.

Graph Layout

The common Picture Controls standard allows for the presentation of Picture Controls as coordinates on a grid, with saturation as the horizontal axis and contrast as the vertical axis. Because of this, you can see the connections between the picture controls you've chosen and the rest of the interface.

(*Contrast is the sole metric displayed in monochrome.) When you're making adjustments, pressing the [Thumbnail/Playback Zoom] button will switch to a grid view.

This will show you the picture controls saved in your camera as relative coordinates for contrast and saturation.

In contrast to the slider display shown on the Picture Control adjustment screen, the grid display, which adheres to a common Picture Controls standard, shows the positions of contrast and saturation. Despite both settings appearing as o on their respective Picture Control adjustment panels, it becomes evident with use that Standard and Vivid do not have identical

Contrast 0 and Saturation 0 values. (*Contrast is the sole metric displayed in monochrome.)

With the optional Camera Operation Pro 2 that allows remote operation of Picture Control, as well as Nikon ViewNX 2 or Capture NX 2 incorporating the Picture Control Utility, the Picture Control System can be further upgraded with software.

You can edit and process raw NEF files and do basic editing using ViewNX-i or Capture NX-D on Nikon cameras and DSLRs that came after the D810 (June 2014).

Picture Control Utility 2 is a free application that may be used with either ViewNX-i or Capture NX-D. It supports the FLAT picture control and allows you to use picture controls while working with these products.

Personalized image controls

With the help of custom picture controls, you can design and give each picture a unique look. You can also use Picture Controls to make Picture Control Utility, which is accessible through ViewNX 2 or Picture Control Utility 2, which is launched from within ViewNX-i or Capture NX-D. Alternatively, you can import picture controls made on other cameras onto your memory card and register them as your own custom picture controls.

You can also alter and register custom picture controls in the camera. They are renameable, deleteable, and memory card-copy-able. You can import custom picture controls made with Picture Control Utility and register them in your camera, and you can freely share files between cameras or photographers via a memory card.

In addition, you can use the Picture Control Utility to transfer custom picture controls made in your camera to your computer. Then, you can use ViewNX 2 or CaptureNX 2 to apply these controls to your images. Or, if your camera is newer (released after June 2014), you can use Picture Control Utility 2, which is accessible from within ViewNX-i or Capture NX-D. Please refer to your camera's instruction manual to get the exact number of configurable picture controls. Picture Control Utility 2: Primary Purposes and

Features

Management of user-created picture controls: adding, removing, renaming, and importing custom picture controls from and into the picture control list and memory card are all part of user-created picture control management.

You can tweak the saturation, sharpness, contrast, and brightness of non-monochrome picture controls while seeing the changes reflected in a live preview of a sample image.

The picture controls for monochrome images let you change the brightness, contrast, and sharpening, as well as apply filter effects and tone. You have the option to either overwrite or save as new the picture controls that you have modified; in either case, the original software's picture control function will automatically reflect the changes.

Make simultaneous changes to brightness and contrast with bespoke tone curves instead of adjusting each slider individually.

You can import pre-made tone curves into Picture Control Utility or make your own.

Sony Vegas Pro 2

You can use the Picture Controls for [Image Adjustment] to modify any NEF (RAW image format) file.

Adobe Photoshop CS 2

By navigating to Develop > Camera Settings > Picture Control, you can apply Picture Controls to any NEF (Netherlands Open File Format) file. Similar to how you can modify custom picture controls in Picture Control Utility, you can likewise modify custom tone curves. Even raw picture (NEF) files captured by older models, like the D2XS, can be processed using picture controls.

Digital Camera Manager 2

When a Nikon DSLR camera with Picture Controls is linked to a computer over USB, the Processing Panel of the Camera Control Pro panel allows you to choose and configure the Picture Controls.

The Adjustment Dialog opens when you press the [Edit] button, letting you make changes to the presently chosen Picture Control. You can rename or remove the camera's custom picture controls from the Custom Picture Control Dialog that appears when you press the [Custom Picture Control] button.

Listen to NX-i

Navigate to ViewNX-i's File menu, then choose Launch Picture Control Utility to get Picture Control Utility 2. Before working with NEF (RAW) files, Picture Control Utility 2 allows you to revert to the Picture Control setting you had before shooting.

Nox-D capture

To access the second version of the Picture Control Utility, open Capture NX-D and navigate to the Tool menu. When working with NEF (RAW) files, Picture Control Utility allows you to alter the picture control that was chosen while shooting.

Chapter 6

Body Design and Connectivity

An expansive 3.2" 1.04m-dot LCD screen is at your disposal for live view filming and bright, clear, and vivid image playback. The screen is tilted to accommodate working at low or high angles, and it's touch-screen for easier navigation, settings control, and operation.

At eye level, you'll find an electronic finder with a 3.69-meter dot.

For quick and effective photo and video file saving, the two SD card slots each support protocols up to UHS-II.

Working in severe weather or dusty environments is easier with a sturdy magnesium alloy chassis. The camera has built-in Snap Bridge connectivity, which allows for the easy transfer of low-resolution images, and it also has remote shooting capabilities.

The camera can communicate with a smart device through BLE (Bluetooth Low Energy) and Wi-Fi, and the smart device can also trigger the shutter and show the live view image from the camera, allowing for remote work.

You get around 470 shots out of the included EN-EL15c rechargeable lithium-ion battery on a single charge, and you can charge it inside the camera using the USB port—yes, even while it's on. If you want even more shooting time, you can attach the optional MB-N10 multi-battery power pack.

Additional capabilities of the camera Dream, Morning, Pop, Somber, Dramatic, Silence, Bleached, Melancholic, Pure, Denim, Toy, Sepia, Blue, Red, Pink, Charcoal, Graphite, Binary, and Carbon are some of the creative picture controls.

There are a plethora of exposure options that can be used to creatively merge many exposures into a single frame.

You can take up to 300 consecutive images in Focus Shift mode, with the focus position moved with each shot. These can be stacked into one image with extended depth of field, which is great for close-ups of smaller objects, landscapes, and other still subjects.

The new EN-EL15C battery powers the Z5, and it supports USB PD, so you can charge the camera with a portable battery pack. The MB-N10 grip, which is used on the Z6 and Z7, is also compatible with the Z5.

Conclusion

The Nikon Z5 is without a doubt the best camera currently available. Its 24MP sensor produces slightly subpar images compared to the best in its class, and the design, ergonomics, and build quality are all inherited from the more expensive Nikon Z models.

The autofocus is also very good, and the camera's dependable face and eye detection make it an excellent pick for capturing family and friend portraits.

The Z5 is capable of capturing 4K/30p video, albeit with a 1.7X crop. 1080p video, on the other hand, makes use of the entire sensor area without cropping.

Unfortunately, the Z5 does not have any high-speed settings, such as 120 fps. It comes with a headphone and microphone port.